FORGIvE THEM
FOR THEY KNOW NOT
WHAT THEY DO

DEALING WITH GRIEF

KATHY ZACKS

TRILOGY
A WHOLLY OWNED SUBSIDIARY OF **TBN**
PROFESSIONAL PUBLISHING MEETS POWERFUL PROMOTION

Trilogy Christian Publishers
A Wholly Owned Subsidiary of Trinity Broadcasting Network
2442 Michelle Drive
Tustin, CA 92780
Copyright © 2024 by Kathy Zacks
All Scripture quotations, unless otherwise noted, are taken from THE HOLY BIBLE, NEW INTERNATIONAL VERSION®, NIV® Copyright © 1973, 1978, 1984, 2011 by Biblica, Inc.® Used by permission. All rights reserved worldwide.
Scripture quotations marked ESV are taken from the ESV® Bible (The Holy Bible, English Standard Version®), copyright © 2001 by Crossway Bibles, a publishing ministry of Good News Publishers. Used by permission. All rights reserved.
Scripture quotations marked (YLT) are taken from the 1898 Young's Literal Translation of the Holy Bible by J.N. Young.
Scripture quotations marked (KJV) are taken from The Holy Bible, King James Version. Cambridge Edition: 1769.
All rights reserved, including the right to reproduce this book or portions thereof in any form whatsoever.
For information, address Trilogy Christian Publishing
Rights Department, 2442 Michelle Drive, Tustin, CA 92780.
Trilogy Christian Publishing/ TBN and colophon are trademarks of Trinity Broadcasting Network.
For information about special discounts for bulk purchases, please contact Trilogy Christian Publishing.

Trilogy Disclaimer: The views and content expressed in this book are those of the author and may not necessarily reflect the views and doctrine of Trilogy Christian Publishing or the Trinity Broadcasting Network.

10 9 8 7 6 5 4 3 2 1
Library of Congress Cataloging-in-Publication Data is available.
ISBN 979-8-89333-743-3
ISBN 979-8-89333-744-0

TABLE OF CONTENTS

FOREWORD 7

TRUE LOVE IS ETERNAL EVERLASTING
CAN BE ONE SIDED IS UNCONDITIONAL 9

LIFE AFTER SPOUSE. 15

THINGS TO DO WHILE YOU'RE TRYING TO
PROCESS. 19

NOTHING CAN CONTAIN LOVE. 23

JESUS, MY BEST FRIEND FOREVER 27

FORGIVE THEM FOR THEY KNOW
NOT WHAT THEY DO 45

ABOUT ME 63

CONCLUSION. 67

ENDNOTES 69

FOREWORD

First off, this book is dedicated to the One who created me = JESUS.

Secondly, I dedicate this book to all my friends and family.

I have three Facebook pages, one personal and two for ministry. I really don't like social media, but I use it as a way to share Scripture.

One of my favorite movie stars is John Schneider from *The Dukes of Hazzard*. I happened upon his Facebook page one day. It was soon after his wife, Alicia, had gone to be with our Lord. His letters to her were, and still are, very deep, romantic, and you can tell that he truly loved and adored her. This is something that I don't find in many marriages. The romance side of things kind of goes astray. Anyway, please check out his Facebook page and thejohnschneider.com. He has some interesting products. I occasionally check back to see if the book that he has been working on is finished. I told him to get his "love letters" published. They are so refreshing to read and get to the point of this heart and gut-wrenching journey we call "Grief."

Please of course pray for our nation, the world, and first and foremost, trust in God. Also, please keep in prayer the brokenhearted. Grief is something that people don't like to discuss much...hence, the elephant in the room. It's sometimes too painful to talk about, let alone think about.

TRUE LOVE IS ETERNAL EVERLASTING CAN BE ONE SIDED IS UNCONDITIONAL

"True love is a unique and passionate bond that connects you as a couple and that wants the best for the other person, regardless of what that means for them. It is the foundation for a healthy, loving relationship. True love is authentic and genuine."[1]

True love according to the Bible: "Love is patient and kind. Love does not envy or boast. It is not arrogant or rude. It does not insist on its own way. It is not irritable or resentful. It does not rejoice at wrongdoing, but rejoices with the truth" (1 Corinthians 13:4–8, ESV).

Difference Between Love and True Love

Love—one can let go, move on, find a new second love.

True Love—dedication—sacrifice your life for that special someone.

Pure Love in a Relationship

Pure love is unconditional. It's kind, compassionate, generous, and nurturing. It's warm and forgiving. It's freely given without expectations of reciprocation. Pure love costs nothing to give, yet it seems like loving one another, loving ourselves, and loving our world is hard to do right now.

True love happens when you fully accept your partner. You don't try to fix or change him/her or turn them into a different person.

Three Main Qualities of Love

Passion—refers to the intense physical attraction partners feel toward one another.

Intimacy—a familiar and very close emotional connection with someone. It requires communication, honesty, vulnerability, and reciprocity.

Commitment—an agreement or pledge to do something in the future.

    a. Affective Commitment—affection for a job

    b. Continuous Commitment—fear of loss

    c. Normative Commitment—sense of obligation to stay

Levels of Commitment

1. Self-awareness—aware of new ideas. A new skill you want to develop.
2. Willingness to change—most people get stuck here.
3. Intense Focus
4. Commitment
5. Character

The purest form of love is loving someone the way they are and loving them until your last breath without expecting anything in return. Your heart has to be pure and your intentions must be true. Only then can you say that you are blessed enough to feel that love in your life for someone.

Appreciation

Appreciation is the purest, strongest form of love. It is the outward-bound kind of love that asks for nothing and gives everything.

Five Stages of Love

1. True love stands the test of time, distance, and absence, making it grow stronger.
2. True love never ends.

And now these three remain Faith, Hope, and Love. But the greatest of these is love.
1 Corinthians 13:13 (NIV)

3. LOVE MUST BE SINCERE.

Let love and faithfulness never leave you, bind them around your neck, write them on the tablet of your heart.
Proverbs 3:3 (NIV)

There is no fear in love; but perfect love casts out fear. For fear has to do with punishment, and whoever fears has not been perfected in love.
1 John 4:18 (ESV)

In this the love of God was made manifest among us, that God sent His only Son into the world, so that we might live through Him. In this is love, not that we have loved God, but that He loved us and sent His Son to be the propitiation for our sins.
1 John 4:9–10 (ESV)

4. LOVE EACH OTHER.

My command is this: Love each other as I have loved you.

John 15:12 (NIV)

5. LOVE AT ALL TIMES.

Do everything in Love.

1 Corinthians 16:14

A friend loves at all times and a brother is born for a time of adversity.

Proverbs 17:17

For God so loved the world that He gave His one and Only Son that whoever believes in Him shall not perish but have eternal life.

John 3:16

Does True Love Need to Be Reciprocated?

Good love is freely given, with no expectations of return. You can reciprocate love without fully accepting it first.

If love is not reciprocated, you may feel rejected and worry that you are unworthy of their affections. This can lead to isolation.

Real love is when you can be yourself and know that your partner accepts you for who you are.

True love can happen many times.

What Does the Bible Say About Widows?

The widow who is really in need and left alone, puts her hope in God and continues night and day to pray and to ask God for help.
1 Timothy 5:5

Honor widows that are widows indeed.
1 Timothy 5:3

A father of the fatherless, a defender of widows, is God in His Holy habitation.
Psalm 68:5

LIFE AFTER SPOUSE

1. Take care of yourself.
2. Try to eat right.
3. Talk with caring friends.
4. Visit with members of your religious community.
5. See your doctor.

The Bible says this about death of a spouse:

> *The Lord is near to the brokenhearted and saves the crushed in spirit.*
> **Psalm 34:18 (ESV)**

> *My flesh and my heart faileth but God is the strength of my heart, and my portion forever.*
> **Psalm 73:26 (KJV)**

> *Blessed are they that mourn: for they shall be comforted.*
> **Matthew 5:4 (KJV)**

Stages of Grief

1. Denial
2. Anger

3. Bargaining
4. Depression
5. Acceptance
6. Shock
7. Processing Grief

Three C's of Grief

1. *Choose—choose what's best for you.*
2. *Connect—Connect with others. Socialize.*
3. *Communicate—Be open to talking about it. Be able to express yourself. This may be the hardest part. It's best to talk about it. This is a traumatic experience. One cannot live with this emotion all bottled up inside. Even if you cry while talking about it to yourself, it's still talking. Talking out loud is great, especially when by yourself. Please remember, God hears us at all times, even if we don't know what to say. Crying is an outward emotion of inward pain. It needs to be expressed. Please remember that Jesus wept too. He cries with us. He knows our heart and understands, even when we don't. He made us.*

With grief comes loss of control:

   a. Can't control emotions
   b. Loss of sleep
   c. Loss of appetite

How Long Does Grief Last?

I truly believe it depends on the deepness of the love for the other. We don't get "over" it—we have to go through it daily, hourly, minute by minute.

Shock = usually right after. The one going through this is experiencing what I call "trauma." The person goes numb and shuts down everything. Doesn't want to talk, wants to be left alone. Needs utter silence. Doesn't care what day it is or time. Doesn't want to eat. Wants the nightmare to be over. Feelings include sadness, anger, anxiety, confusion, and depression.

What Can Grieving Do To The Body?

Grief can cause inflammation, joint pain, headaches, and digestive problems. It can lower your immunity, making one susceptible to illness.

THINGS TO DO WHILE YOU'RE TRYING TO PROCESS

1. Journal—Journaling is very important.
2. Set up a chair and have coffee and just sit and talk. Make this a standard each morning, noon, or night—or whatever.
3. Please remember—You are never ALONE. Jesus is with you. We can't see Him either—but we know that we know HE is there. It's the same. We know our loved one is with us. They have never left.
4. GO DO—Bless others, talk about it. It's okay to cry—Buy plenty of Kleenex and hankies; carry them with you always and take them to bed.
5. Pamper yourself—Go eat out, get a facial, a pedicure, buy something special for yourself. Play sports, go golfing, or whatever it is that you like to do.
6. Find a grief class where you can talk about it. One size doesn't fit all.
7. Be creative—I love arts and crafts, crocheting, singing, playing piano and guitar. Set up rooms that are totally you.

8. Meditate on His Word—sometimes just BE STILL and know that He is God. He's the best.

9. PRAY—always pray. I pray for the heaviness in my heart to go away. For that void or that hole to close.

10. Think of the Greatest Love = JESUS. I think of Him often in the garden sweating blood. I don't think it was sweat. I think His body was crying, weeping tears of blood. I think His body was shutting down before the Cross. The thought and the weight of our sins were so immense. I truly believe that when it rains, it's His tears. He cries and mourns for the lost, the evil, the corruption. Don't forget HE made us—BEAUTIFUL MASTERPIECES. He knitted us completely in the womb and He left a gold threat to complete us = JESUS. Please look up LAMININ. You will see the sign of the Cross in every cell. His love for us is so very deep.

11. Remember—Jesus is very close to us, especially to the brokenhearted. He feels our pain. He knows and understands, even though we don't.

Love is full of empathy and compassion. It never fails. It's never ending. Love is exhilarating. Love is passionate. Love is kind. Love is generous. Love is JESUS. Love is your spouse, friends, cat, dog, and so forth. Love is the greatest emotion. Love is deeply felt. Love is painful. Love hurts. Love sucks sometimes. Love is pure. Love is everlasting. Love is enduring. Love is unconditional.

Love can be frightening. Love can be crazy. Love can be passionate. Love can be fulfilling.

LOVE CAN _____ (you fill in the blanks).

LOVE IS _____ (you fill in the blanks).

NOTHING CAN CONTAIN LOVE

In my way of thinking, there is no vessel that can truly contain the magnitude and depth of love. Our bodies were not made to hold it...to contain it. The depth of it is so powerful that one cannot truly hold it. That is why I think we can't control it, especially when a loved one is no longer there. A loved one can be any living thing. The heart of a person I believe is tied to their soul. With the heart, one can love much.

One has to have a pure heart to see God. What does this mean?

Suicide

I tried to commit suicide twice by the age of twelve, once at nine, and again at twelve.

Suicide is prevalent on my mom's side. My grandma and my sister both died of suicide.

I, myself, have lost track of how many times I did this—it's probably at least twenty times.

Please remember that SUICIDE is a PERMANENT solution to a TEMPORARY problem. However, your way of thinking at that time is only one way out. It's dark—you're alone. You feel abandoned, deserted, like everything is your fault. The only way out...is out. If you're contemplating suicide, please get help! Joyce Meyers calls it "stinky thinking," which it is.[2] God makes each day new for a reason.

Please remember that the past is the past. We cannot change the past. JESUS can change today and make a brighter tomorrow and future.

Please understand that Jesus is my best friend.

I am not proud of my attempts at taking myself out. The last attempt I remember is quite vivid. My husband, at the time, and I were going on vacation to Florida, I believe. We were living in Georgia and I had my three children in the back of the car. I was the navigator. We had reservations and what was supposed to be a three-hour trip turned out to be six. Every time I told him to turn right, he would turn left. The reservation was for 6:00 p.m. We arrived at 7:30 p.m. We were driving up to the hotel; it was dark; it was late; the kids were hungry; everyone was on edge. He started yelling at me and there was a 50-foot drop or so off of my side—no railing. I opened the door and was going to jump. My middle one was crying, "Mommy, don't go, please Mommy, don't go!" The other two were sobbing.

Well, we made it to the hotel. We got some food and it was never mentioned again.

Even though I believed in JESUS and was saved, I turned

to alcohol, prescription drugs, and suicide as an escape.

It wasn't until I found out my husband was cheating on me that I fully surrendered out of total desperation. JESUS delivered me, not only from myself, but from the addictions. I was pain free. My back didn't hurt anymore. I was T-boned in an accident about three or four years earlier. I also had panic attacks, severe bouts of depression, and anxiety—which were all generational curses. I was classified as mentally ill before I surrendered everything to JESUS. JESUS is in charge of my life now. I am so glad HE's in charge because I can really screw things up on my own.

JESUS, MY BEST FRIEND FOREVER

Let me tell you, when JESUS saves you...HE saves you. My biggest enemy was myself.

I was afraid of myself...my mother's rejection, my rape when I was a virgin and subsequent abortion, my car accident going through a windshield and hitting a telephone pole at two years of age with no broken bones, no stitches, NOTHING. My first husband did Russian roulette on me, strangled me, and said I wasn't breathing. I had died and went to heaven and came back. Mother Superior, after high school, stated that I had "a higher calling on my life." I had wanted to be a nun after graduating from high school. My other husbands were abusive. One clocked me in my jaw and loosened my teeth, and they started falling out. I felt alone and afraid.

I was lost and JESUS found me where I was—picked me up, dusted me off, and said, "YOU'RE MINE." I have been HIS ever since. I have seen my guardian angels. They are huge. Totally decked out. Their swords are huge and they have thousands of angels "dressed to kill" to protect me. When afraid, please pray that you can see your guardian angels. When we see them and how many angels there are behind them, well, you're not afraid anymore.

If He does this for me, I know He can protect you too. I often forget to read Ephesians each day, so I prayed that He would cover my armor too, each and every day. I feel totally blessed and heavily guarded.

In 2002, my children and I moved to Las Vegas, as this was to be my mission field. I started feeding the homeless by myself and evangelizing on the streets of Vegas as soon as I was situated. I found a church in Vegas (VBF) in (I think) 2005 or 2006. I met Ron, who was an ex-addict living out on the streets of Vegas (homeless), and he started a ministry. I was eager to join his ministry. He eventually got into the Salvation Army on Owens Street in Las Vegas. We had twenty-five people to feed when it first started. I think for six months I cooked, led worship, and occasionally would preach/teach. I usually gave my testimony and then did altar calls. Prayer was always offered.

I cooked for the homeless for almost four years until it reached 150 and I couldn't do it by myself anymore. Funds were tight and I couldn't afford it. This was about 2017.

Prayer

Our communication with our Creator (Father) is through prayer. Many of us have set up war rooms. We need to understand how the enemy operates in order to defeat him at his schemes—to keep him at bay. *WAR ROOM* is a great movie. We need to pray 24/7. Most of the time we end up on our knees. When I think of prayer, I think of the picture of George Washington kneeling beside his horse.

Praise and Worship

Praise facilitates access to God. "Enter His gates with thanksgiving and His courts with praise" (Psalm 100:4, NIV).

The definition of praise is to glorify God.

God says this about praise: "Through Jesus, therefore, let us continually offer to God a sacrifice of praise—the fruit of lips that openly profess His Name. And do not forget to do good and to share with others, for with such sacrifices God is pleased" (Hebrews 13:15–16, NIV).

Why is praise important to God? It's a purposeful way to invite God's presence. God wants to hear us, our words, our cares, and our heart. The Bible states that God inhabits the praise of His people (Psalm 22:3).

Seven Types of Praise

Towdah—sacrifice of praise

Yadah—hands raised

Barak—quiet voice

Halal—soul rejoice

Zamar—instrument song

Tehilah—sing along

Shabach—shout for joy

Seven Components of Praise

1. Praise is positive
2. Praise reinforces high expectations
3. Praise is appropriate
4. Praise promotes independence
5. Praise is sincere
6. Praise notes effort and progress
7. Praise can be a great motivator

> *Praise God in his sanctuary; praise him in his mighty heavens. Praise him for his acts of power; praise him for his surpassing greatness... Let everything that has breath praise the Lord.*
> **Psalm 150:1, 2, 6**

> *Praise gives us access to God. "Enter His gates with thanksgiving and His courts with Praise.*
> **Psalm 100:4 (ESV)**

Praise is a powerful weapon—it is used in deliverance and spiritual warfare. It can help tear down strongholds. I suggest that if you are going through grief, that you pray, praise, and worship the King of Kings and Lord of Lords = JESUS.

David praised God because he knew that God was keeping him safe and guiding him.

I praise Him because He saved me. He left the ninety-nine to find me. He never gave up hope on me, even though I gave up hope on Him. I thought that He had let all these things (terrible things—rejection, rape, abortion, lies, and deception) happen to me because He hated me so very much. He couldn't stand to look at me—or be around me. That all was a lie from the pit of hell.

I was like Jacob. Jacob had it out and fought an angel of God and lost. God always wins. When He wins, He wins BIG TIME!

Worship

First off, what is worship? This is the definition: "Worship is when we give our deepest affections and highest praise to something. True worship of God is when we love Him with all our heart, soul, mind, and strength. It's when we prize God above everything else and put Him first in our hearts."[3]

"The Lord our God, the Lord is one!" (Deuteronomy 6:4–5, ESV).

I know from experience that God can shut down a gift if it is not used with His intent. He shut me down in high school when I opened graduation. It was all about me at that time. I wasn't saved at that time. I heard, "If you don't use what I have given you, I will shut it down." He spoke this to me three times at my high school graduation. If I don't use my voice for His glory, well, it will get shut down permanently. He gives us gifts, especially music, to reach the lost. I truly believe music was created to help heal one's soul.

I know throughout my childhood, music was my go-to. I truly didn't understand the depth of it at that time. I understand it now. Music transcends the soul. Lucifer, before he was cast to the fiery pit, was the most beautiful angel and the lead musician. He thought that he was better than God. Pride is such an evil spirit and something that I had to deal with early on. I came to realize that I could not function at all if it wasn't for Him breathing life into me continuously. Think about it. Every time we breathe, He breathes. It's amazing. Breath in Hebrew is *Ruach*. In the beginning, He breathed life into every living being. I often read Genesis and am blown away each and every time. I find a nugget or two when reading and am amazed at how much He truly loves us even though we fail Him daily.

Dreaded Days

Shortly after my husband's death, I tried going back to church. I got the stares, pats on the back, and all the rest.

I placed my Bible on the empty chair beside me and the flood pursued. I picked up the Bible and ran. You see, years prior, since 2004, I had put the Bible down next to me to pray for a godly man. The chair was empty until I married.

How We Met

He would open the prayer room at church and we would talk afterwards. That happened for about six months until he disappeared. I didn't think anything of it until about two years later when I heard he was divorced and had moved to Mississippi.

We talked for hours on the phone each day and looked forward to the discussions about JESUS. He would always pray before we hung up each and every night.

He proposed to me over the phone and I accepted. He eventually moved back to Vegas and we got married in May 2017. We separated in May 2018. I had the marriage annulled in 2019 and he passed in October 2020 due to a stroke.

I had three months of the godly man, prayer in the morning and at night, going to church, date night on Wednesdays, flowers, and so forth. The addiction to steroids is what killed our marriage, along with his trumpet playing. He never put God first. Everything that he wanted to do came first. I was last. He never hugged me or wanted to be close to me. He saw me on the sofa crying and just shook his head and went into the bedroom.

I never knew that steroids can affect not only one's appearance, but it can change their attitude and demeanor.

He said he loved me, but his actions showed otherwise. It came down to one night when he threatened to hit me and take me out (meaning kill me). That's when I knew our marriage was completely broken. I asked him to go to counseling with me. He said, "No, I will not subject myself to pastors or men." I told him he had to leave and that this house serves the Lord.

Pity

What is pity? Have you ever had a real-life pity party? Well, I have. I have stayed in my pity parties way too long.

There are two different definitions for pity:

1. sympathetic sorrow for one's suffering, distressed or unhappy compassion.
2. something to be regretted, it's a pity you can't go.[4]

Let's go with definition number two. God suggests in Psalm 13 resisting self-pity by crying out to Him in humility, trusting in God's love, and rejoicing in salvation.

I must say, I gave really good pity parties. The biggest word was, "IF." IF I had only done this or said that before they died. I didn't do this right to him/her, so therefore, this is what God will do to me, etc.

I believe it's okay to have a pity party...just don't stay there. God wants us to be happy. The JOY of the Lord is OUR strength. He wants us to be happy no matter what. Pick yourself up off the floor, dust off your shoulders and say, "I can do all things through JESUS who gives me strength" (Philippians 4:13, KJV). He died for our sins so that we don't have to relive them day in and day out. Please remember, WE ALL FALL SHORT. Sometimes the shorter becomes the longest. He knows us the best. He created us with all the intricacies. We are like prize jewels going through the polishing phase. We get ground, polished, put back in a solution to get the specks out, and go through the different phases over and over again. He wants us to shine like the face of Moses when he came down from Mount Sinai. Amazing what Moses went through with the burning bush and all. He wants us to be consumed in Him just like that burning bush that never fades but keeps on burning day in and day out.

I never wanted sympathy or pity. When I found out he was gone—really gone—I went through every little thing asking God, "Did I do what was right? Was I a godly wife? Had I dotted my *i's* and crossed my *t's*?" Did I do it His way or my way?

Being an ex-addict, I know what it's like to now live with a familiar spirit. We are to love that person and hate the spirit, right? Forgive and turn the other cheek, right? I went through anger and depression—it seemed simultaneously. I had known this man for two years before we got married, and another almost two years of marriage equals four years. He lived on his own for about a year or so, suffered a stroke and then was gone. I felt used and betrayed.

I have my AA in music. Steve played the trumpet. He would play the scales over and over again so loud...I think he was deaf.

I forgot the name of the band that Steve was in. He was pretty famous back in the seventies. He left school when he was sixteen to go on tour. He went to Japan and overseas. He not only played in the band but was also their road manager. They lived in a van or in hotels. He never had to clean. Thus, he never liked to clean the house at all. He would say it would just get dirty. I needed a comeback and so I prayed. I heard, "Ask him why he takes a shower? He will still get dirty"...lol. I was left to do everything I did before the marriage. Now, I was cleaning and tidying up after him as well.

I enrolled in medical school because I knew I needed to take care of my parents. At this time, I was going to school full time and working part time. My health started deteriorating because of the stress.

We eventually stopped sleeping together. I gave him the bed and I slept on the sofa. I would cry myself to sleep with his dog, Romeo, on my belly. Romeo was a chihuahua. He also had a Maine Coon cat named Sampson. Steve couldn't see well enough to clean out the litter box. I put in the bags, which made it easier to clean. He had never cleaned out the litter box with soap and water. By the time I got to it...well, it was pretty gross. Don't get me wrong, I am not perfect.

I don't believe that anyone is perfect except God, Jesus, and the Holy Spirit. I am imperfectly perfect. We are all made in His image. We all have a conscience, whether we choose to listen to it or not. He gave us free will. There's no dictatorship in heaven. He is extremely jealous. I guess I would be too. Along with jealousy, on the other side of the spectrum is passion, love, and being zealous in everything one does.

Each Day is New

Please remember that each day is new. JESUS made each day new for a reason. Forget the past. We cannot change the past. The past is done and over. However, JESUS made each day new so that we would have a new hope, new dreams, new visions. Please remember during this time to take care of you.

I moved away from family and friends in Vegas—Florida is now a new adventure. I had suffered from PTSD in the past where I locked myself in the room each day and wouldn't go out. I find that I can do new things by myself—I can learn new things and venture out. I like visiting art museums, or museums in general. The enemy doesn't want you to go out. He doesn't want you voicing your opinion. He doesn't want you spending time reading your Bible or speaking the Word of God. I realized that I have the ability to overcome certain things. I just purchased a trike bicycle. It was supposed to be a 7-speed but it's not. Getting out of the house/garage and getting on it is something I need to overcome gradually. I wish I could lock it up outside. Out here in Florida there are a lot of bugs and I am afraid I would have to clean off the bike or sit on bugs...yuck.

Nothing Ever Completely Dies

There's always rebirth or new life. Even when we go home to be with our Lord JESUS we are renewed—rebirthed. Though our loved ones no longer feel pain and are hopefully with our Lord—they have a new body, new perspective, and a total understanding of our Lord JESUS, our Father, and the Holy Spirit. I truly believe that all newborns have a total understanding of love and that they crave and desire it, even in the womb.

We will get a full tour of the heavens when we go to be with Him.

There's no holding back—there will be a tour of the Milky Way, stars, planets, galaxies, music, choirs, angels, plants... everything He created.

Please remember that what we see here on Earth is just

a glimpse of heaven. The colors are brighter, the streets are of gold, and New Jerusalem will have huge gates and precious stones.

Our brains were created in such a way to process very, very—did I say very small portions of Kingdom values, riches, and glory. He knew we couldn't comprehend it all, but it awaits us.

Our spirits will be in full alignment with the Creator of heaven and earth forever. That sounds so glorious. What a beautiful concept. I cannot wait.

What is Long-Suffering?

The Lord is not slack concerning His promise, as some men count slackness, but is long suffering to us-ward, not willing that any should perish, but that all should come to repentance

2 Peter 3:9 (KJV)

The love is long-suffering, it is kind, the love doth not envy, the love doth not vaunt itself, is not puffed up, doth not act unseemly, doth not seek its own things, is not provoked, doth not impute evil. Rejoiceth not over righteousness and rejoiceth with truth. All things it beareth, all it believeth, all it hopeth, all it endureth. The love doth never fail, and whether there

> *be prophecies, they shall become useless; whether tongues, they shall cease; whether knowledge, it shall become useless.*
> **1 Corinthians 13:4–8 (YLT)**

God made us to give love—love isn't an option. Love is a gift which makes love much easier to give than to receive.

JESUS had to leave and pray to our Father in order to receive love since He gave His Love freely. That's why we need to be connected to HIM to get recharged.

HEARTBROKENNESS

What is heartbrokenness? Heartbrokenness means full of sorrow. It is expressed by or marked with sorrow that is associated with irreparable loss.

What does the Bible say about heartbrokenness?

> *The Lord is nigh unto them that are of a broken heart: And saveth such as be of a contrite spirit. Many are the afflictions of the righteous. But the Lord delivereth him out of them all. He keepeth all his bones: Not one of them is broken. Evil shall slay the wicked: And they that hate the righteous shall be desolate. The Lord redeemeth the soul of his servants. And none of them that trust in him shall be desolate.*

> ## Psalm 34:18–22 (KJV)
>
> *He heals the brokenhearted and binds up their wounds.*
> ## Psalm 147:3
>
> *He will wipe away every tear from their eyes, and death shall be no more, neither shall there be mourning, nor crying, nor pain anymore, for the former things have passed away.*
> ## Revelation 21:4 (ESV)

My favorite:

> *The Lord is close to the brokenhearted and saves those who are crushed in spirit.*
> ## Psalm 34:18
>
> *You keep track of all my sorrows. You have collected all my tears in your bottle. You have recorded each one in your book.*
> ## Psalm 56:8

This is just a sample of what God can do to heal you. I have learned that sometimes healing can be a process, especially when it comes to heart issues. The enemy will use any weapon that he has to get your mind off of God. Oh, believe me, I have gone to the depths with the enemy because of pain. However, I have learned to not dwell on the pain as much. I have to refocus myself and dwell on the One that made me. He should always be our focus throughout the day.

I know this is hard to do. I raised three children by myself. I had two to three jobs at a time, trying to bring in enough money to sustain my small family. It was hard. It was gruesome. However, I do not know how I managed to do everything. All I know is that JESUS walked me through it. I always trust Him now. I can screw up anything. However, when I surrender everything to Him each day, it's a whole lot easier. I never ever want to go back to the days of when I was popping pills and drinking enormous amounts of alcohol.

I get so mad at psychiatrists who just prescribe pain medication. All that doctor is doing is putting a Band-Aid over a bleeding artery. It doesn't solve the issue. JESUS is the answer to all things.

To those who are hurting. First off, I am so very sorry that you are going through this. The pain of missing someone that was just there and is not there physically any longer can be devastating, to say the least. It is the most hurtful experience that anyone can go through. JESUS went through that with Lazarus. I truly believe that JESUS was crying because those that were grieving didn't receive the message of eternal life. We have everlasting life with JESUS. JESUS knew that He would raise Lazarus from the grave. He wept because He saw them heartbroken. They thought they would never see their brother and dear friend ever again. I truly believe that JESUS sent us the Holy

Spirit to comfort us in this time of grief. He knows and understands heart issues.

TRIALS AND TRIBULATIONS

I truly believe that we are tested, tried, and purified. No test, no testimony. The greater the test, the greater the testimony. Nothing ventured, nothing gained. I believe He wants to make sure we believe and trust in Him totally. I also believe that every completed room in our mansion is a completed test.

This journey of grief is a test—a test of long suffering at times, a test of purity of heart, a test of selflessness, a test of humility, and the list goes on and on. The harder the test, the bigger the rooms. Each day, each hour, though we miss them dearly—I am thankful that JESUS is here to wipe the tears, comfort me, and say, "Get up, we need you." So, I digress, so that He can impress those with His compassion, grace, mercy and, most importantly, "LOVE!"

The harvest is full but the laborers are few.

LIVING IN THE LAST DAYS

According to the Bible, we are living in the last days. Our duty is to get His Word out.

I don't need a crown nor want a crown; I don't deserve

a crown. I believe what Paul said—He died for me and that's the least I can do for Him. That's how I feel—I don't need a mansion. I need to be sitting at His feet like Martha and being a sponge. Just being there in heaven with Him is plenty. I heard the buffets are stupendous!

We will all know each other, not by name, but by the fullness of our spirits. We will gravitate towards each other as we gravitate towards Him. He will always remain the center of our attention and focus.

TIME DOESN'T STOP

Time doesn't stop—it didn't stop when JESUS died. Why should time stop? Life goes on—even though we feel we can't. It comes in waves, like a roller coaster—continuous. Grief is an unwelcome friend who doesn't know when to leave. It's rude—it just enters without knocking and leaves very seldom, but takes a lot out of us. The pain swells up inside so intensely that one thinks they may explode. The tears well up and then, "bloomin' blunders," it's flood time. We just sit and wait for another swell, not knowing when or where it'll happen, but it does.

FORGIVE THEM FOR THEY KNOW NOT WHAT THEY DO

"Forgive them for they know not what they do" is what I heard today. Hence, the title of the book. It's really hard to forgive someone over and over again. It doesn't get easier. In my opinion, it becomes much harder, especially when you know someone is being deliberate. Forgive always, forgive constantly. Love and bless those who hurt you. Pray for them. Pray, praise, and worship our Lord JESUS without ceasing.

Difficult Times With Family And Friends

Trying to get through grief is an experience in itself. Trying to remain calm while friends or family start taking your inheritance is a bit unnerving and unsettling.

I am writing this book while taking care of our mom and trying to cope with the passing of our dad. I am handling the medical and legal aspects. It's really hard when one person goes rogue and tries to take away everything that our parents left us just because they have power of attorney. I don't like powers of attorney. I think if left in the wrong person's hands, well, it can be devastating. Hence, this is what is going on.

I am just very thankful that God equipped me with medical and legal experience. I am still very humbled that He would have me write this book. A lot of pain and emotions were orchestrated to write this book. Just remember, He always has us go through something terrible in order to help someone else. We are NEVER alone. HE is ALWAYS with us.

FLORIDA

I moved to Florida to hopefully spend my retirement with friends I had known for seventeen years. When it came down to the move from Vegas to Florida, they blatantly told me not to come. I wasn't welcome. My son, Jonathan, wasn't too happy about me leaving him in Vegas. We had never been separated since he was born.

Another God story is the trip to Florida. I moved with no contract in place. No deposit was secured. I found out that new management in Florida came in April and that they threw out the waiting list that had hundreds of names on it. I'm on a fixed/low income and had applied at many places, but prayed and God sent me to fill out an application in May, and I was to get my place at the end of June. I had tried to book a car rental for the end of June but there were none. I had to take a Lyft ride from Tampa to Crystal River, Florida. I had only been to Miami and Disney World in Florida. I had never heard of Crystal River. Crystal River is located approximately an hour and a half northwest of

Tampa.

I thought it was funny that my driver was asking me for directions. I left Vegas at 11:00 p.m. and arrived in Tampa, Florida around 6:00 a.m. I was tired because I had been up since 3:00 a.m. to get everything thrown out in Vegas and packed. My huge luggage was too heavy for me to pick up. I had a large suitcase that weighed just under fifty pounds and my carry-on weighed about thirty pounds.

There was a beautiful family that saw how I was struggling and carried my bags to Starbucks, where I was able to sit down and get a banana and some coffee. I hadn't eaten since 3:00 p.m. Vegas time. I wasn't able to eat too much because I was so excited to start my new life...or so I thought.

It was really hard packing all my things up. What do you take? What do you leave behind? I had just bought a brand-new bed. It was a canopy bed. I had always wanted one when I was little. I thought it was cool and strung some lights on it. It was my war bed. This is where I prayed. I donated a lot of things to neighbors, friends, and family. I sold my car and was using that money for the first couple of months to live. I thought I would have enough money for savings. I had only secured a bed frame, box spring, mattress, and pillow before I arrived in Florida.

I arrived at the rental office early to fill out the paperwork. They quoted it incorrectly, and I had to pay more money. The unit was supposed to be ready at 3:00 p.m. They tried to deliver my bed at 1:00 p.m. They had to come back and were eventually able to set it up. The unit wasn't ready until 5:30–6:00 p.m. The cleaning lady was there until 8:00 p.m. I was handed the keys by the manager. She just dropped me off, handed me the keys, and went on her merry way. There was no walk-through.

The place was huge. It had all wooden floors. It was in a natural setting. There were palm trees all over the place. It looked like it was set in a jungle. There was a park next door. It was a three bedroom, two bath, with a huge one-car garage. The unit had a washer and dryer in the garage, but the dryer didn't work. I ended up drying the clothes in the garage. The office was a full three or four streets away. The streets were long.

One day I was walking early in the morning. I think it was around 5:00 a.m. It was still dark. I saw a black figure rise up over the mailboxes. At first, I thought it was a black jaguar or something of that nature. It turned out to be a black bear with a cub. I just froze and waited for them to cross into the woods. I stayed there completely frozen for a few moments. I was trying to figure out what had just happened. I realized the mail wasn't that important and walked slowly home. I wasn't sure if the bear was tracking me or not.

I had no car and realized that I would have to depend on public transportation. There was only one bus that ran from 8:00 a.m. until 3:00 p.m. Monday through Friday.

PALMETTOS

Oh my, let me tell you about the bugs in Florida. I thought they were huge in Georgia. However, I had never seen a flying cockroach. This thing had the belly of a bumblebee and lunged right at me. I took off my shoe, and that sucker was deader than a doornail. It flew right towards me. I had seen several other ones, but they were dead.

The carpenter ants were another unwelcome guest. I was covered with them. I think they got hooked onto my long nightgown. I woke up to what was like a nest of them. It was terrible. I had to wash my night gown five times before they came out. My legs were all bit up. The bites were worse than fire ants. Their stings lasted for days. I had to put makeup on my legs so that no one would think I had a terrible disease.

LOOKING BACK

Looking back, I was a very afraid little girl. I was afraid of everything, especially God. I really thought He was very angry with me. I had seen *The Ten Commandments* several times and thought that God was going to strike me down at any moment. I figured I had done something so very wrong that He hated me. He was disgusted with me. He didn't want to see my ugly face anymore. He was fed up with me...just like my parents. That was a bunch of lies that the enemy had me believing for years. It wasn't until I got saved that I felt His unconditional love.

THIS IS WHAT HAPPENED AT CHURCH ON THE WAY IN VAN NUYS, CALIFORNIA.

I didn't want to go to church anymore. I was dragged to church my whole life and where, really, where did it get me? I became indignant and overly confident in the world. I was conniving. I would throw people "under the bus" all day long in order to get to another rung on the corporate ladder. I didn't care about anyone except myself.

However, one day I listened to the call of going back to church. I had always loved listening to Pastor Jack Hayford. I had seen him on television a few times. I decided to go one Sunday morning. All I remember is that I was standing there during the altar call. When I stood up, I was immediately lifted into the air by thousands of angels. I had never, ever felt so much love in my entire life. I just remember the usher coming up to me and asking me if I was okay. I looked down and nodded to him. That was the best day of my life. I never looked back. Everyone at work noticed that I had changed. My heart went from cold to sometimes overly emotional. That's okay with me. I would rather be this way than the other any day.

DO NOT LEAN TO YOUR OWN UNDERSTANDING

"Trust in the Lord with all thine heart; and lean not unto thine own understanding. In all thy ways, acknowledge

Him, and He shall direct thy paths" (Proverbs 3:5–6, KJV).

HOW TO TRUST IN GOD

1. Be honest.
2. Seek out truth in the Word of God.
3. Share your concerns with others.
4. Be still and spend time with Him. He is bigger than ANY circumstance.
5. Always be grateful.
6. Always listen to the Holy Spirit. He's a chatterbox.
7. Always, always, wait on JESUS.

TRUSTING GOD COMPLETELY

1. Know who God is.
2. Know His heart and intentions.
3. Surrender everything to Him.
4. Have a lot of patience

Sometimes we don't understand completely why things happen or why God allows things to happen. I do know we SERVE a loving God and maybe, just maybe, He missed them too and saw how sad they were or saw their health failing.

Have You Ever Taken Care Of Someone On Hospice Or Who Did Not Have Long To Live?

I have several times. My best friend, Gail, had Stage IV cancer. It went from uterine to colon, to breast, and then lung. She was diagnosed with cancer in her twenties. She lived to be sixty-four. She taught me about herbs.

My sister, Linda, went to the hospital to have a cyst above her eye removed. She was twelve years old. She was given the last rites of the Catholic Church three times. She went into rehab to learn to walk, eat, and go about her daily activities. I learned to do physical therapy on her when I was fourteen or fifteen.

Now, I am taking care of my parents. Even though they were very abusive, God brings everything around 360. My dad didn't make it to his ninety-fourth birthday. He was a week shy of it. My dad did teach me a lot. Most importantly, he taught me about being compassionate and having empathy. He taught me to be able to be strong and to stand on my own. I grew up in Chicago and learned how to fight from him. When we moved to California, in the eighth grade, I was given the title of "Golden Gloves."

Today

It's hard dealing with the stress of knowing our mom can

go at any moment. I am the one doing the legal work for the family as well. I have contacted every agency possible and still nothing.

I have learned from counseling that hurting people hurt other people. Angry people have a lot of pent-up unforgiveness, and because they are hurting, they try to put it on you. That is why I believe that I was given this book to write so that people would understand that we need JESUS more and more each day. We need HIS LOVE. This is why it's important to forgive and forgive often. But most importantly, forgive yourself. You did the very best you could do given the circumstances.

Being a Caregiver

Being a caregiver is one of the hardest things one can do. I am in a position where it has been 24/7 nonstop. I truly believe I was born a natural caregiver. I was raised to take care of everyone first. I would always eat last.

Caregiving can be the most rewarding and also the most unappreciative job one has to do. It requires selflessness, which the world nowadays doesn't seem to appreciate or recognize.

Having taken care of both my parents, I can say my dad, who I miss dearly, was always very appreciative. His eyes would light up when I said or called him "my daddy."

My mom, on the other hand, can give "zingers" in a straight shot to the heart. She complains all day long. That's Mom.

I guess the most important thing is a caregiver is a servant. We always think of others first.

Being a chaplain, I always put myself in the other person's shoes and always think about What Would JESUS Do, in every situation. Love, compassion, empathy, and so forth are gifts from above. No one is better than anyone else. The love of money is the root of all evil. Money can't buy happiness. One cannot take everything with you when you die.

I have met billionaires, some with inherited wealth and some that started with nothing. They have remained humble. Please remember that what God gives, HE can also take away.

You Got the News

Well, you got the news that your loved one(s) is going to pass soon. Some don't get the news. They're just not here any longer.

I dated a Vietnam vet for five years. His wife sent him a "Dear John" letter. They had two small sons. He was divorced while he was overseas. He could not see his own sons until they were much older. She was having an affair and had gotten remarried.

Grief can happen to anyone, anywhere, at any time. How does one prepare? You don't. One is never prepared for someone that you love being gone forever or until they meet you in heaven. Our minds don't match up with the heart's pulls and tugs.

You scream, shout, "It's not fair! Why, God, why?" We may never know why. I believe everyone is sent on an assignment by God and, once completed, He calls us home.

I have had too many things happen to me—venomous bites, loaded guns held to my head, strangled and left for dead, a knife pulled on me, someone tried to drown me—I know I have a purpose and that's to spread HIS WORD and love on as many people as possible.

Marriage God's Way

Today, everyone wants to sleep around. It's like buying a car. One has to test it out before they purchase it. However, that is not God's way. God created Adam and Eve, not Adam and Steve. If he only created men or women, there would not have been YOU.

According to HIS WORD, one should not lie with another until they are married. When God created marriage, it was to be with one man or one woman for life. Nowadays, it seems as if when one doesn't agree with the other person, they file for divorce.

I can tell you from experience, one of the hardest divorces was when I found out my husband was sleeping with someone else. The trust was gone. I could no longer look him in the face. He had hurt me so profusely. He had been doing it ever since we were married. I believe with two or three other women. I had to move on. I couldn't cope. He was the one that filed for divorce and got remarried.

It's Not a Loss, It's Absent

Definition of absent: "not present in a place or at an occasion."[5]

Definition of loss: "a person or thing that is badly missed when lost."[6]

Definition of lost: "unable to find one's way; not knowing one's whereabouts. A defeat that has been sustained."[7]

Definition of emptiness: "the quality or feeling of being without significance or purpose; meaninglessness."[8]

I have a hard time when someone comes up to me and says "I am so sorry for your loss." To me, I know where my loved one is. They're not lost or missing. They're just gone from this world into the arms of JESUS.

Saw this on Facebook

This is probably the best answer I have ever heard to the

question, "Why did God create evil?"

A professor at the university asked his students the following question: "Everything that exists was created by God?"

One student bravely answered, "Yes, created by God."

Did God create everything? The professor asked.

"Yes, sir," replied the student.

The professor asked: If God created everything, then God created evil, since it exists. And according to the principle that our deeds define ourselves, then God is evil.

The student became silent after hearing such an answer. The professor was very pleased with himself. He boasted to students for proving once again that faith in God is a myth. Another student raised his hand and said, "Can I ask you a question, Professor?"

"Of course," replied the professor.

The student got up and asked. "Professor, is cold a thing?"

"What kind of question is that? Of course it exists. Have you ever been cold?" Students laughed at the young man's question.

The young man answered. "Actually, sir, cold doesn't exist. According to the law of physics, what we consider cold is the absence of heat. A person or object can be studied on whether it has or transmits energy. Absolute zero (-460 degrees Fahrenheit) is a complete absence of heat. All matter becomes inert and unable to react at this temperature. Cold does not exist. We created this word to describe what we feel in the absence of heat." The student continued. "Professor, does darkness exist?

The professor answered, "Of course it exists."

"You're wrong again, sir. Darkness is actually the absence of light. We can study the light but not the darkness. We can use Newton's prism to spread white light across multiple colors and explore the different wavelengths of each color. You can't measure darkness. A simple ray of light can break into the world of darkness and illuminate it. How can you tell how dark a certain space is? You measure how much light is presented. Isn't it so? Darkness is a term man uses to describe what happens in the absence of light."

In the end, the young man asked the professor, "Sir, does evil exist?"

This time it was uncertain. The professor answered: "Of course, as I said before, we can see it every day. Cruelty, numerous crimes, and violence throughout the world. These examples are nothing but a manifestation of evil."

To this, the student answered. "Evil does not exist, sir, or at least it does not exist for itself. Evil is simply the absence of God. It is like darkness and cold—a man-made word to describe the absence of God. God did not create evil. Evil is not faith or love, which exist as light and warmth. Evil is the result of this absence of Divine love in the human heart. It's the kind of cold that comes when there is not heat, or the kind of darkness that comes when there's not light."

The student's name was Albert Einstein.[9]

Happiness is a Choice

God has given us the opportunity to choose to be happy, sad, glad, cry, and so on. These are all choices. I choose to be happy...most of the time. I do have my sad moments. For the most part, I choose happiness. My feeling is that JESUS died for us so that we can be happy if we so choose. To not be happy is not living in the abundance of what HE has given for us when HE died on the Cross for us. HE not only died for our sins, but HE died so that we can have grace, mercy, peace, happiness, joy...and the list goes on and on. I know that in these circumstances that joy and happiness doesn't seem to go with the picture. Oh, see so and so, her husband just passed and she is so happy...hardly. The life I had being married is long gone. It's a whole lot of faded memories that just don't add up with how I am feeling today.

Do I miss my husband? Definitely. I need to adjust again to the single life. Eating alone in restaurants used to make me queasy. I enjoy ordering food and having it delivered. Dating is just not something that I automatically jump in to. I find dating just a horrible, what I call either a "hit or miss." At my age, it's usually a "miss." I need to focus on God and dig deeper into what HE is all about.

I have noticed that the deeper you go into HIS WORD and meditate on it, HE sends you a lot of fish. You can catch more fish in deeper waters than you can close to shore.

Material Things that Bring Memories

I notice some people have a whole treasure trove of a prior loved one's items and things. They have treasure chests full of those things that bring back enjoyment, good times, songs, and memories. I think those are great. Those are just not me. Right now, I am living in my parents' home. Everything right now speaks to me of my dad. I just miss him terribly. He always used to make me laugh and vice versa. It's really hard to imagine right now me living somewhere else. I know we will have probate once Mom passes and then from there, who knows? I know I will end up with family.

There are certain items that remind me of my dad. Every time I drive his car, the tears, or "bloomin' blunders," start to fall. I pray that the Lord will keep me safe.

I remember all the times my dad would sit next to me and I'd say, "Let's lock and load." My dad was seventeen when he joined the Army. He was stationed in Pearl Harbor after the Japanese attacked us. Dad was always a jokester, and I always figured he was joking when he said he was stationed in Hawaii with "hula" girls.

It's sad to think that something of great value, a "prized possession," would be stolen. John Schneider just posted that the General Lee, which his wife purchased for him, was stolen, along with the Corvette he purchased for her. These gifts of love to each other were very thoughtful, but "PRICELESS." I don't understand how people can be so cruel—hence, again, the name of the book.

What Have You Got to Lose?

Well, I heard a pastor say that the favorite song played in hell is the song "I DID IT MY WAY."

If you are struggling with life, trying to erase pain, hurtful events, feel abandoned, feel rejected, feel unloved, or just a plain nuisance, TRY JESUS. What have you got to lose?

Being an ex-addict, almost in prostitution, abused and so all alone—I truly thought God hated me and left me to die. I thought I could speed up the process by self-infliction—take myself out of the equation. That was never the intent.

JESUS loves you so very much that He sent His only Son to die on a Cross—a horrible death, to pay for our sins. His love is everlasting, long-suffering. He endured what no one should ever have to endure for all of mankind. He died for ALL.

My prayer is that you repent of your sins and accept JESUS

FORGIVE THEM FOR THEY KNOW NOT WHAT THEY DO

to be your Lord and Savior. We can't do life without Him, we can't breathe, eat, go to the restroom, walk, talk, etc., without Him.

He created you and knows you a whole lot better than anyone else. Surrender your life today to Him. Watch TBN and download the app on your phone. Find a church, get baptized to show everyone how much you love JESUS. READ, READ, READ, and PRAY without ceasing. This world is ugly. This world is full of sin. JESUS wants us to be a light to this world. To spread HIS TRUTH.

You won't ever be the same or have the same friends. He made you new. One has to be born again in order to enter the kingdom of heaven. That's found in the book of John.

First of all, I want to welcome you personally, dear brother and sister, if you did the above. Please write to me at chaplainzacks@gmail.com if you have any questions or concerns. Please contact a suicide hotline or get a hold of someone immediately if you are contemplating suicide. Suicide is NOT an option. There's so much work to do before the rapture.

Most importantly, please remember that JESUS loves you and so do I.

"Pray for a peace that passes all understanding. Blessed are those that mourn, for they shall be comforted" (Matthew 5:4, ESV).

ABOUT ME

I was ordained a chaplain in 2016. I am a certified addiction and abuse recovery coach. I have my AA in music, and my BA from San Diego Christian College in Human Development. I am a certified paralegal from California. I went to school for medical billing, medical transcription, medical assistant, and X-ray.

I was saved in April 1988 at Church on the Way in Van Nuys, California.

I was physically, mentally, and emotionally abused from birth. I am the eldest of six children. Only five are still living.

I was disowned over thirty years ago by my parents because of my beliefs. I was raised Roman Catholic and went to parochial school for twelve years.

I was a virgin when I got raped at twenty years of age. I got pregnant and had an abortion. I spiraled further into deep despair. I had low self esteem.

I married four abusive men. The first marriage was the worst. He would get drunk, load his 357 Magnum with hollow points and pull the trigger. Finally, the gun jammed. I believe that an angel was sent to deliver me. He choked me and I had an out-of-body experience. I truly believe I was dead. He left after I stopped breathing for ten minutes. God gave me another chance. Otherwise, I would have gone straight to hell. He is the God of many, many, many, and more chances.

I had gone to Christian counseling and my counselor told me that what really hurt me most was being the eldest and not being able to help my siblings. I could barely take care of myself. I believe I was to be the protector of the family. I was an adult at age six. I was treated as such and in all the decisions of the family. I quickly realized that what my parents were doing was wrong. I stood up and took the blows.

I was addicted to alcohol at the age of eight years old. I started drinking to ease the pain. I tried to commit suicide twice by the time I was twelve years of age. I was diagnosed with PTSD after the Northridge earthquake. I was put on meds and quickly became dependent on those instead of God.

I couldn't stand the pain any longer and cried out to God to deliver me from everything. I couldn't go on living like this anymore. God delivered me from everything...being afraid, drinking, drugs, everything. I realized that I cannot do anything without JESUS. He breathes when we do. HE is my everything.

I moved from Georgia to Las Vegas in 2002. I stayed in Vegas until June of 2022. I moved back to Vegas to take care of my parents. Boy, what a 360. God's Word says to honor your mother and your father, period. It doesn't say only if they were good. God sent me back to Vegas for a reason and a purpose. It was to get to know my parents and to help them in their time of need. My dad passed away in February of 2024. All my siblings still live in California, so I don't have much help physically but have all the help I need spiritually. He sends people to minister to me. My mom was admitted to hospice in October of 2023, and I moved back to Vegas September 11, 2023. I had been taking care of both parents until January of 2024 when Mom was placed into a facility. We brought Mom back home the day after Dad died.

It has been hectic, to say the least. Forgiving doesn't mean that you need to forget as well. I guess I will always remember the disappointment in how I was raised. However, that doesn't mean that I have to go on living with it. There was a lot of anger stored up between God and I. Like I said, I had a Joshua moment. Please remember that God always wins. There is nothing that JESUS won't do for you. Always remember to thank Him for everything and put Him first in all things.

I pray that those who read this book are blessed. Pray without ceasing and be ready to go home soon. I believe the Rapture will soon be upon us. We need to ask JESUS to keep our hearts pure and to make sure we have enough oil in our lamps.

FORGIVE THEM FOR THEY KNOW NOT WHAT THEY DO

Even though we may not have a father and mother who love us unconditionally, please remember that we have a wonderful Father in heaven that totally does. He totally gets us. He made us and therefore knows how we feel and why we act the way we do. JESUS loves you so very much.

CONCLUSION

The once extremely frightened little girl isn't frightened or afraid anymore. I suffered from high anxiety, diagnosed with PTSD in 1996. I had been traumatized most of my entire life.

God delivered me from all of the addictions, the pain, low self-esteem, and turned me into a Mighty Warrior for His Kingdom.

I just want to let you know that if JESUS can do this for me, He can do this for you too. I am no one special. I don't have any special gifts on my own. It is only through His power and might that I can survive each and every day. Please read Ephesians on fighting in the Spirit.

These are the things to win the battle each and every day.

1. Put Him first above all things.
2. Pray without ceasing.
3. Surrender daily. He guides your steps each day. Listen to the Holy Spirit.
4. Remember to pray for you too.
5. Pray, Praise, and Worship. Put on some great worship CDs or the radio. Out here, SOS is a great place to listen to worship music.

6. Please forgive and forgive often.

I pray that this book will bless you and will help you deal with GRIEF. The key is that you are not alone. Also, you are not alone with vultures at the door trying to get what they don't deserve.

Please remember that God is faithful, just, and merciful. Most importantly, JESUS loves you.

I pray that this book will enlighten your path. A path that is very treacherous at times. Thankfully, you don't have to do it alone.

Great blessings to all. May your days be filled with joy and happiness as we remember those who will always be a part of us, no matter where we go or what we do. God bless.

ENDNOTES

1 "What Is True Love?" Novembere 14, 2021. The Loveteam. https://en.lovebox.love/blogs/news/what-is-true-love.

2 Joyce Meyer Ministries. 2021. "Stinking Thinking | Joyce Meyer." YouTube. June 5, 2021. https://www.youtube.com/watch?v=WPRsdpEr5kY.

3 "What Is Worship according to The…." n.d. Love Worth Finding Ministries. https://www.lwf.org/gods-desires-for-you-a-biblical-guide/what-is-worship-according-to-the-bible#:~:text=Worship%20is%20when%20we%20give.

4 "Definition of PITY." 2024. Www.merriam-Webster.com. July 3, 2024. https://www.merriam-webster.com/dictionary/pity#:~:text=pity%2C%20compassion%2C%20commiseration%2C%20condolence.

5 "Absent | Encyclopedia.com." n.d. Www.encyclopedia.com. Accessed July 25, 2024. https://www.encyclopedia.com/literature-and-arts/language-linguistics-and-literary-terms/english-vocabulary-d/absent.

6 "Loss | Encyclopedia.com." n.d. Www.encyclopedia.

com. Accessed July 25, 2024. https://www.encyclopedia.com/social-sciences-and-law/law/law/loss.

7   "Lost | Encyclopedia.com." n.d. Www.encyclopedia.com. https://www.encyclopedia.com/humanities/dictionaries-thesauruses-pictures-and-press-releases/lost-1.

8   "Dictionary.com | Meanings & Definitions of English Words." n.d. Dictionary.com. Accessed July 25, 2024. https://www.dictionary.com/browse/emptiness.

9   "Facebook." n.d. Www.facebook.com. Accessed July 14, 2024. https://www.facebook.com/photo.php?fbid=853612199909245&id=100057814189933&set=a.172395808030891&locale=cs_CZ.

Printed in the USA
CPSIA information can be obtained
at www.ICGtesting.com
LVHW050424291024
794996LV00011BA/123